January 1975

Brenda Robinson,

With many thanks

for many happy hours in

your classroom.

Hilary Sherlock

Ears and Tails and Common Sense

Ears and Tails and Common Sense

MORE STORIES FROM THE CARIBBEAN

by Philip M. Sherlock
and Hilary Sherlock

Illustrated by ALIKI

THOMAS Y. CROWELL COMPANY   NEW YORK

BY PHILIP M. SHERLOCK
Anansi the Spider Man:
Jamaican Folk Tales
The Iguana's Tail:
Crick Crack Stories from the Caribbean

BY PHILIP M. SHERLOCK
AND HILARY SHERLOCK
Ears and Tails and Common Sense:
More Stories from the Caribbean

Designed by Meri Shardin and Aliki

Manufactured in the United States of America

Library of Congress Cataloging in Publication Data
Sherlock, Sir Philip Manderson.
    Ears and tails and common sense.
    SUMMARY: During each evening of their eight-day party the forest animals listen to a story told by the animals who guess the answers to Chimpanzee's riddles. 1. Tales, West Indian. 2. Animals, Legends and stories of. [1. Folklore—West Indian. 2. Animals—Fiction] I. Sherlock, Hilary, joint author. II. Aliki, illus. III. Title. PZ8.1.S54
Ear   398.2′45   74–2045   ISBN 0–690–00450–8

I   2   3   4   5   6   7   8   9   10

For Samantha,
first grandchild and first niece

Contents

The West Indies

N

C O C E A N

VIRGIN ISLANDS

UERTO RICO

Anguilla

St. Kitts

Barbuda

Nevis

Antigua

Montserrat

Guadeloupe

C E A

Dominica

Martinique

St. Lucia

St. Vincent

Barbados

Bequia

Grenada

Tobago

Trinidad

E L A

Where Do the Stories Come From?

It is sunset time and story time on the island of Tobago. Boys and girls stand on the sandy beach and watch the sun dip into the ocean far away in the west. One of them tries to find the first stars in the pale sky. Another climbs onto the low branch of an almond tree and watches the tiny waves as they whisper gently to the land. Nearby an old fisherman sits on the bow of his dugout, his pirogue he calls it, mending his nets. The light is fading, and as more and more stars appear in the sky, the old man throws down his net, lights his short clay-stemmed pipe, and calls out,

> "Riddle me riddle, riddle me ree,
> Guess me this riddle and perhaps not."

Before he can finish the lines the boys and girls have gathered around him, some sitting in the canoe, others at the foot of the almond tree. "Tell the riddle, tell the riddle," they shout, and the game of guessing begins.

It is sunset time and story time in Martinique also. There the boys and girls speak French, for that is the language of the island, as it is also of the neighboring island of Guadeloupe. In a village at the foot of the sleeping volcano, Mt. Pelé, the children gather in front of the cottage of Tante Lucie, Aunt Lucie. Some are night black, others golden brown, others a rich chocolate brown, others fair of skin, just like the boys and girls in Tobago, Jamaica, Trinidad, Barbados, and all the other fifty-one inhabited islands of the Caribbean Sea. One calls out, "Time for a Crick Crack story, Tante Lucie, time for a Crick Crack story," and while silence falls and the night shadows creep over the land, Tante Lucie begins.

"Crick Crack"

And the children say,

"Break my back."

The map gives a picture of the islands of the Caribbean, the lands from which these stories come. Like a bright rainbow the islands curve from the giant-sized island of Cuba, through middle-sized Jamaica and Puerto Rico and smaller islands like Guadeloupe, Dominica, Martinique, St. Lucia, St. Vincent, Barbados and Grenada, all the way to Tobago, Trinidad, Curaçao, and Aruba. Clustered around these there are handkerchief-sized islands like the Virgin Islands and Montserrat and mini-mini islands like Bequia, which is only a few miles wide.

Rainbow islands they all are. Their names have a touch of magic, just as a rainbow fills the sky with magic. Tobago is the name that the Arawaks, its first dwellers, gave to the island. It means tobacco, tobacco island. Haiti is also an old Indian name. It means mountainous land. Jamaica is another old name, meaning land of wood and water. There are newer names also, like those that Christopher Columbus gave to the islands more than 400 years ago. As he sailed toward one of them he saw three mountain peaks close together against the sky and he cried, "Three together, a trinity of mountains. That is the land of the Trinity, Trinidad." It was Sunday when he found another island, to which he gave the name Dominica, after the Spanish word for Sunday, Domingo. When he sailed through the cluster of little islands off Puerto Rico he said, "These are like St.

Ursula and her group of ten thousand virgins," and he called them the Virgin Islands. On another island was a mountain peak which seemed to carry a smaller peak on its shoulder. "That is St. Christopher carrying the Child Jesus across a river," he said, and he named the island St. Christopher. We call it St. Kitts for short.

Rainbows are lovely because they combine many different colors, all the colors of the spectrum: green, blue, yellow, red, indigo, violet, and orange. The islands of the Caribbean, like a rainbow, combine differences of race and skin color and language. Many of the people of the Caribbean are black and they have their origins in Africa. Others are white, with their origins in different parts of Europe, mostly in Spain, France, and the British Isles. Some have skins with the delicate tint of old ivory. Their forefathers came from the Far East, from China. There are brown-skinned people from India, olive-skinned people from the Middle East, and people of mixed race.

There are differences of language too, and differences in the way of life, in the styles of building, in the methods of cooking. In the islands of the Netherlands Antilles, like Curaçao and Aruba, Dutch is the language, and the older houses are built with high gables as in Holland. As we have seen, French is the language of Guadeloupe and Martinique and other islands of the French Antilles. Here the houses and churches are built in the style of France and, as in France, most of the people are Roman Catholics. In nearby Barbados, however, the language is English and just as London has its Trafalgar Square, so does Bridgetown, the chief city of Barbados.

Though there are differences, it is easy to see that the islands belong to the same family. They all grow crops of bananas, sugar cane, oranges, and coconuts. They all have the same out-of-doors way of life and they all share the same sea, the Caribbean. And in all the islands they play the riddle game and tell folktales about animals.

The stories may be told in different ways from island to island, and characters who are very much alike may have different names. For example, the stories about Anansi the Spider Man are told in Jamaica and Haiti and in many of the islands of the eastern Caribbean. In Jamaica the Spider Man keeps the name Anansi, which is the name he has among the Ashanti people of Ghana in Africa. But in Haiti, which is French-speaking, he is Ti-Jean, which means Uncle John. In the islands of St. Lucia and Grenada, where the language of the people is based largely on French, he has yet another name, Compé Czien.

Compé is short for Compere, and the name means Brother Spider.

Also stories may be known in some islands but not in others. In Jamaica, for example, *most* of the folktales are Anansi stories. In other islands of the Caribbean the tales tell of a number of different animals and are called Crick Crack stories.

The differences are not greater than family differences, though, and the stories are alike in several important ways. They are not about giants and sleeping princesses and fairies, but about animals. Sometimes men and women appear, but for the most part the characters are animals like Anansi, Tiger, Rabbit, Cat, Goat and the others. The animals behave as we do, and the stories, full of sunshine, poke fun at human failings such as greed, selfishness, and vanity, things that deserve to be laughed at.

As we listen to the tales, we remember that black people in the United States also have their rabbit stories and that throughout West Africa people tell folktales in which animals are the chief characters, animals such as Tortoise, Rabbit, and Spider. We can see how the stories and riddles of the Caribbean link the boys and girls of those islands with boys and girls in other New World countries and with those in Old World places such as Nigeria and Ghana. The stories form a part of the rich rainbow beauty of mankind.

Brown Owl Plans a Party

Green Parrot wanted to whisper her very special idea to Little Capuchin Monkey. She wanted to whisper it knowing that especially good ideas always start as whispers. The trouble with Green Parrot was that she found it difficult to whisper. As hard as she tried her softest whisper was a loud croaking in her throat. So when she tried to whisper her idea to Capuchin Monkey he jumped and almost fell from the tree. He put his paws to his ears and then took them away quickly, for he seemed to be just trapping the noise inside.

Capuchin Monkey screwed up his face. "That sounded just like a hacksaw going at full speed. The next time you want to tell me a secret you had better sit about three yards away and whisper from there."

Green Parrot's feathers drooped. "But then anyone nearby could hear and it wouldn't be a secret, would it?" she said in a surprisingly quiet voice.

Capuchin smiled slightly at Green Parrot. "I'll come a little nearer, Parrot. Speak as softly as you can, and please, don't get too close to my poor ear. Go gently with it. It's still aching inside."

Green Parrot felt better immediately, and she turned her head to Capuchin Monkey and winked. She had the most complete wink in the forest. She had an eyelid that was perfect for winking. It moved across her eye just as if it were a window blind going slowly down and up again.

"Tell me your secret, Green Parrot. I can't understand *everything* by your wink language."

"We should have a party," said Green Parrot.

"Whose birthday is it? Not yours and it certainly could not be Chimpanzee's. He never lets anyone forget that his is in January."

"It's nobody's birthday, but it's everybody's birthday," Parrot croaked, smiling a very secretive half-smile.

"Nonsense, what day could be nobody's birthday and everybody's birthday. You are talking back to front this morning."

"All right, Capuchin, I'll give you a clue. How long is it since the long march?"

"Oh!" Capuchin smiled. "I understand now. Let me see. . . . We set off from our old home in the dry season when everything was parched. That was at the end of September. . . ."

"And what month is this?" asked Parrot. She beamed, nodding her head in a most excited fashion.

"Of course! What a splendid idea. We should have a party. It is one whole year since the march. How quickly it has gone. We must not forget that we have not always lived here. Let's find Brown Owl and see what she thinks."

"It's too early for Brown Owl. She's inclined to be very grumpy if awakened so early. We really ought to consult Chimpanzee first," Parrot replied. "He was our leader on the march and if we are going to have a celebration we must talk to him first."

"Yes, we'll let Brown Owl sleep for a while longer and go to Chimpanzee first, but you know, if he likes the idea he's going to believe he thought it up himself."

Parrot and Capuchin Monkey set off. Capuchin swung along from treetop to treetop, stopping only now and then to pick a small ripe berry or a tender green shoot. Parrot shot off quickly, skimming over the leaves. She moved like a flash of changing

colors through the sky. Capuchin, pausing to chew a berry, looked up at her and thought, "She is like a bit of rainbow that's broken loose. But what a whisper she has, what a hacksaw whisper."

Green Parrot arrived at Chimpanzee's first. When Capuchin Monkey got there he could hear her explaining to Chimpanzee, "You can be chairman of the party." They all knew that Chimpanzee liked to be in charge of things.

Chimpanzee looked pleased. "You may be a little bird, but you do have some brains in that tiny head of yours. Let's make our plans. We must have a plan and you know who is good at planning—Brown Owl. It's time she was consulted."

"But she is asleep and you know how she is just after she wakes up."

"Chimpanzee snorted. "I'm with you. It will be all right."

They went to Brown Owl's home, a little hole in a tall tree. Looking in they could see she was fast asleep, her big eyes tightly closed. Then she jumped and looked puzzled. Was her tree falling? Gradually she realized that it was just Parrot whispering her name. She opened her eyes and moved slowly to the doorway, blinking as the light grew stronger.

"I can't come any farther, the light is much too bright. What do you want, Parrot?"

"We want you to make a plan for us, Brown Owl. You are so good at it. Go back into the dark and listen. I will explain," Chimpanzee said softly.

Brown Owl knew what they wanted immediately. She thought back to when they had left their other home. For weeks and weeks the sky had always been blue and the sun silver, so that the earth grew hard and the plants withered. They had had to find a new home, a place where there was plenty of food and water. She remembered the long march when hot sand filled the air and heat waves ran across the brown earth. That was a year ago. Yes, they must have a party, and it would be a good party with riddles and stories.

"Excellent idea, Chimpanzee! How clever you are."

"Well, Brown Owl," replied Chimpanzee, "Parrot did help a little, just a little, you understand."

Parrot winked at Capuchin Monkey. What did it matter if Chimpanzee thought the party was his idea? He would work with them so that it would be a good celebration.

"Now," said Brown Owl, "time for serious

planning. A one-year celebration for all of us must last a week and a day. If it were for one of us then the party could be just one day long, but since it is for all of us it should last a week and a day. That's just right, one week and one day!"

"Good," said Chimpanzee. "I have never been able to understand your arithmetic myself, but I like your idea. What shall we do during the week to make it special?"

Brown Owl told them of her plan. "Every evening we will gather at Chimpanzee's house and tell stories, just as we did on the march."

"And riddles, we must have riddles too. I love riddles. I will tell the first story." Green Parrot chattered excitedly.

"Hold it." Brown Owl laughed. "Just a minute. We will use the riddles to decide who will tell the stories. Chimpanzee will tell six riddles in all. On the first evening of the party, he will tell three and those who guess the answers will tell the first three stories."

"Suppose the same person always guesses the riddle?" Little Capuchin Monkey asked.

"Once you have guessed correctly you are not allowed to try again," Brown Owl replied.

"I think this is a good plan," said Chimpanzee.

"Green Parrot and Capuchin, you go around the forest and tell everyone that Monday evening when the sun begins to set, we'll meet in the clearing at my home. And you can invite Hacka Tiger, but tell him I'll be keeping an eye on him."

As they set off, Chimpanzee, since he was a very careful person, shouted after them, "And each animal should bring his own food."

Riddles One, Two, Three

The morning of the party found everyone in the forest full of excitement. All the animals were busy getting ready for the first night's celebration. Armadillo had had his back polished so that the dark brown shell glowed. Parrot sat preening her turquoise and emerald feathers till they gleamed. Iguana sunned herself and said to Firefly, who sat nearby cleaning his headlamps, "I suppose Hacka Tiger is coming. Do you think it's quite safe for me to go?" She would never forget how Tiger had pounced on her in the forest. Her friends Armadillo, Little Capuchin Monkey and Firefly had helped but she only escaped because, being a lizard, she had shed her tail.

"Quite safe, quite safe," said Firefly. "Chimpanzee is going to watch him and Owl will too."

"All the same I know it will be hard for him to keep his claws off me. I am even plumper than when he last saw me. But I will come with you."

"Let us set off early," replied Firefly. "Remember I must save my headlights for the dark journey back."

The shadows began to lengthen in the forest as the sun fell away toward the far hills. The light softened as Chimpanzee sat waiting for the other animals. He smiled as he heard them coming closer. He could make out Capuchin's chatter, Parrot's squawk, and Owl's hoot. He also heard Iguana's shuffle, and he knew the dainty Firefly would be with her. Chimpanzee was ready, both with his riddles and his appetite, for he would taste a little bit of the food that each animal brought.

Hacka Tiger was one of the last to arrive. He traveled silently on his padded feet. Parrot noticed that Hacka Tiger looked quickly at Iguana, but he sat on the other side of the group. Capuchin noticed that the tip of Hacka Tiger's tail was still. All will be well, he thought, at least for the time being.

There was a burst of chatter as all the animals

called to each other, remembering the long march. They talked of their memories of a year ago, of Armadillo's slowness, Parrot's hoarseness from the dust, Firefly's long rides on Iguana's back.

"Time to begin! Order! Time to begin!" shouted Chimpanzee. "As you all know last September we came here on the long march. It is good here, and we have had a fine year in this, our new home. That is why I decided we should have a party."

Parrot squawked and Chimpanzee coughed and added, "I mean Parrot helped me to think of having a party, a Call-Back-the-March-to-Mind Party. The name is a long one because the party is to be a long one. Oh! And remember to bring your food with you every day."

"The riddles, the riddles," whispered Brown Owl.

"This evening I will ask three riddles. Those who guess these riddles will tell the stories on the first three nights, then on the fourth night I will ask three more riddles for the remaining three nights. Here is the first riddle to begin the celebrations, the Call-Back-the-March-to-Mind Party.

> *Riddle me riddle, riddle me ree,*
> *Guess me this riddle and perhaps not.*
> *Two brothers are ever running a race.*
> *Not one can catch the other."*

"Easy, that's very easy," shrieked Parrot. "The legs of a horse. Everyone knows that."

"Parrot, that's a good try," said Chimpanzee, "a very good try. But the two brothers in the riddle are quite separate. Each one is complete, whereas the four legs of a horse all share the same body. It is such a good try, Parrot, that if no one comes up with the right answer, we will give you a second chance to guess it."

Parrot shut her beak and looked around. She could see all the animals thinking hard. Hacka Tiger's forehead was wrinkled. Iguana's eyes were shut tight. Capuchin sat biting his paw, until suddenly he seemed to remember the riddle from somewhere, somewhere and some other time. He waved his paw in the air and shouted, "The sun and moon, the sun and moon, one never catches the other."

"Right. You will tell tomorrow's story, Capuchin. Now, here is the second riddle.

> *Riddle me riddle, riddle me ree,*
> *Guess me this riddle and perhaps not.*
> *A shower of rain is coming.*
> *There are two empty rooms,*
> *But you cannot shelter in them."*

This time, even Parrot was silent. Hacka Tiger crumpled his brow again and Iguana began to shut her eyes, but catching Hacka Tiger's eye she decided to keep hers open this time.

Armadillo was sitting opposite Chimpanzee. As he thought his eyes wandered over Chimpanzee's face. "Two empty rooms, two empty rooms . . ."

Suddenly that thought became mixed up with, "What a broad nose Chimpanzee has." Nose . . . nose . . . room. . . . The thoughts clicked. . . . "Your nose, your nose, Chimpanzee."

"Not only my nose, not only my nose," shouted Chimpanzee, for he was very sensitive about the shape of his nose. "Everybody's nose, even that tiny beak of a nose that you have. Everyone has a nose and every nose has two empty rooms."

"Truly, Chimpanzee," said Owl, "but Armadillo did get the answer quickly."

"Humph!" snorted Chimpanzee. "All right, Armadillo, you will tell the story on the second night. Now, here is the third riddle.

> *Riddle me riddle, riddle me ree,*
> *Guess me this riddle and perhaps not.*
> *When you are going to town you face town.*
> *When you are coming from town you face town."*

Green Parrot was bursting with the answer. "That's a man climbing a tree."

"How did you get that, Parrot?" asked Capuchin.

"You should have known it too. You climb trees all day. When you climb up your face is turned to the tree, and when you come down your face is still toward it."

"Parrot is right," Chimpanzee declared. "She will tell the third story. Now, Capuchin, remember, we'll hear from you tomorrow evening. Supper now!"

Ears and Tails
and Common Sense

"In the beginning of time," Capuchin began excitedly—

"That's not how to begin. The stories must begin properly," grumbled Hacka Tiger, while Owl hooted, "You forgot something. You forgot something important."

"Sorry, so sorry," said Capuchin.

"Crick Crack."

And all the animals chorused loudly,

"Break my back."

In the first days of the earth when everything was just beginning there were the first animals. They did not look like they do today, for they had no ears, no tails, and even no sense. Each animal had to get his tail from one place, his ears from another, and his sense from yet another. The ears and tails came in different models and sizes, while the sense was kept in a small clay pot.

Rabbit and little Marmoset monkey woke early one morning and set off to get their ears, tails, and their share of sense. They both wanted to find ears and tails that would suit them exactly and, of course, they wanted as much sense as they could hold. Talking the matter over they decided that they each wanted small ears, short tails, and a great deal of sense. In fact, they planned secretly to carry off the pot with all the sense that it held.

They went to the house of the First Elephant, which was hidden deep in the forest near a stream. Here were stored ears in more shapes and sizes than one could imagine. Though they were early several animals had arrived before them. They chuckled when they saw all the confusion. Donkey was try-ing on a pair of pointed ears so small for him that they were quite ridiculous. Goat was prancing around with a floppy pair that made his face look even longer and sadder than it really was. Dog was searching for a pair which he could hold straight

up if he wanted, or flop down, creating whichever effect he desired. Rabbit and Marmoset had to wait. However, when their turn came they did not take long to find what they wanted. Marmoset chose small, dark brown ears. They even had tiny wrinkles to match his crinkly face. Rabbit found a pair that was a little larger than he had originally intended, but he loved their pink insides. He set them back on his head a little, at an angle, so they went with his slanting eyes.

From Elephant's house they hurried along to the house of the First Giraffe who kept a large supply of tails. Rabbit and Marmoset found that they were the first to arrive at Giraffe's house. They took their time and went slowly and carefully through the shelves of tails. They ignored the shelves with the long and medium tails so that they could concentrate on the varieties of small sizes. Rabbit was very pleased with the short uppish tail he found; it went perfectly with his uppish-pointed ears. Marmoset chose a short, brown tail with a little tuft at the tip that made him look quite cheeky.

Now, they set off to accomplish their big task at the house of the First Gorilla. Gorilla was huge, with fierce little red eyes. "If you want a share of

sense you will have to carry out three tasks," he told them. "Everybody must work for his share of sense and that includes you."

Rabbit put on his most timid expression and asked very politely, "What work do you want us to do?" He didn't show his new tail or twitch his new ears for fear of making Gorilla angry. Marmoset kept very still. He knew he was a distant cousin of Gorilla, but he didn't want to take advantage of this. Nobody dared to do that sort of thing with Gorilla.

"Here are your three tasks," said Gorilla. "First get me a gourd full of Tiger Cat's tears. Second, get me a gourd of live wasps, those with red and yellow stripes, the ones we call Jack Spaniards. Third, climb that palm tree with the earthen pot of sense slung around your neck."

"How strange," thought Rabbit. Then, very meekly, he asked, "If I do the first two, can Marmoset do the third? I cannot climb at all, but he can."

Gorilla gave his consent.

Rabbit sat thinking. Every now and then he moved his little tail and scratched an ear. He thought all that day and for half the night. Then he had a little sleep. Early the next morning he set out for the home of the First Tiger Cat, taking with him a piece of paper and a bit of charcoal.

Tiger Cat lived about twelve miles from Gorilla's home. Rabbit found her sitting at the doorway of her house. When he came up to her Rabbit crouched on the ground, put the paper in front of

Tiger Cat and began to make black marks on it with the charcoal. He was very quiet while he was doing this, not even looking at Tiger Cat. After making a number of marks he took up the paper and gave it to Tiger Cat, saying, "Elephant sent this to you."

"You know I haven't learned to read, because I'm so busy. Please read it for me," Tiger grumbled.

"Elephant says that bad times are coming. We shall have what is called a hurricane. The wind will blow so hard it will bend the small trees and snap the tall palms. It will blow away every animal who is not tied tightly to a branch."

"Elephant is a wise man," said Tiger Cat. "He knows all things. Quickly tie me to that tree over there. It's the nearest big and sturdy one."

"I will help you, but we must be quick for I must get back to my hole before the wind comes," Rabbit answered. "Have you got a strong cord?"

Tiger Cat made a fast search and found a length of strong cord. She stood beside the big tree and braced herself against it. Rabbit tied her up, winding the cord around her waist, her legs and shoulders.

"Is that tight enough, Tiger?"

"No, make it tighter," called Tiger. Rabbit pulled

again as Tiger took a deep breath. "It's all right now," gasped Tiger.

Then Rabbit picked up a large stick and began to beat Tiger. "You are stupid," he said. "Obviously you haven't got your sense yet. If you had sense you would know what to listen to and what not to listen to. Elephant should take away your ears from you."

Tiger was so angry she began to howl and cry, not from pain, but from vexation. She was big and strong. Rabbit was small and weak. How ashamed she was that she had been tricked in this way. Rabbit quickly held the gourd under Tiger's eyes and caught the tears, then he hurried off to Gorilla. He was feeling very happy, having completed his first task.

"Now, how am I going to catch a gourd full of live Jack Spaniards?" thought Rabbit. "They are the biggest and fiercest wasps I know, and what a sting they have."

Rabbit found a dry empty gourd. He walked through the forest with it in his hand repeating loudly, "I say 'yes,' I say 'no.'" Owl flew by and when she heard Rabbit saying loudly "I say 'yes,' I say 'no,'" she thought to herself, "Rabbit has stayed in the sun too long and is now quite out of his mind." The First Pigeon flew by, and after listening to Rabbit for a while, went to tell his friend Parrot the sad news that Rabbit was behaving in a most peculiar manner. Blackbird and Armadillo heard him and went away troubled and anxious. After all, what in the world could Rabbit mean muttering "I say 'yes,' I say 'no.'"

Finally Rabbit passed a tree which had a Jack

Spaniard nest on a low branch. The leader of the Jack Spaniards, being the most inquisitive of them all, flew by and hearing Rabbit, buzzed, "What do you mean, walking through the forest like this saying, 'I say "yes," I say "no" '? Why are you behaving like this?"

"Because I met a man," said Rabbit, "and he told me that this gourd can hold two hundred and thirty-four Jack Spaniards. I don't know whether or not to believe him and so, I say 'yes,' I say 'no.' "

"Huh!" said the Jack Spaniard. "We may be small, but we are certainly not that small!"

"I say 'yes,' I say 'no,' " said Rabbit, twitching his nose.

The chief Jack Spaniard buzzed angrily. "I'll prove it. That gourd cannot possibly hold two hundred and thirty-four Jack Spaniards. It cannot, it cannot."

"I say 'yes,' I say 'no.' "

"Well, count then and we'll see. Count while we fly in. I'll make you say 'no' only." A cloud of wasps came flying towards Rabbit. "Follow me," directed the chief Jack Spaniard, "and, Rabbit, you count as we fly in."

"One, two, three, four . . ." Rabbit counted on

and on while the Jack Spaniards flew in one
by one. At two hundred and ten they were all inside the gourd. Rabbit corked it, feeling very
pleased with himself. He had the Jack Spaniards
and he was finished with both the tasks he had to
do. Marmoset would climb the tree. He was good at
that and loved doing it too.

"Let's go for some sense now, Marmoset," cried Rabbit as he shivered and flickered his nose with excitement while his new ears lay back flat against the side of his head.

"Yes, let's go," called Marmoset as he ran halfway up a palm tree just to keep in form.

And so they hurried off to Gorilla. Rabbit handed over the gourd full of Jack Spaniards. "Marmoset is ready for his task. Exactly what do you want him to do?"

"First of all, he must be very careful," replied Gorilla who was in rather a bad mood. "In this earthen pot is kept all the sense that's left in the world. It is not very big for there is very little sense left. You will see there is a cover on the pot. That is to prevent anyone from putting his hand into it. And you know I keep it near me at all times," Gorilla grumbled.

Looking straight at Rabbit, he added, "If anyone were to steal it, if anyone were even to try to steal it . . ." With this Gorilla opened his gulf of a mouth so that Rabbit could look past the chisel-edged barricade of teeth far down to the hungry red throat. When Gorilla bellowed like he did now it made everything and everyone shake. Rabbit almost fell

to the ground and Marmoset trembled at the red
pinpoints of light in the ape's eyes.

Gorilla stamped up and down for about five
minutes. Luckily, a northeast wind blew on him and
he cooled down. "Marmoset, you must climb this
palm tree with the earthen pot around your neck.
Be careful now."

Marmoset set off up the tree with the pot tied
around his neck. The pot began to get in his way.
Whenever he tried to climb, the pot swung back

and forth in front of him. This happened several times. Marmoset was getting angry and worried. "If this wretched thing were not hanging in front of me, getting in my way, bumping about, climbing the tree would be quite easy," he muttered. "Rabbit must be laughing at me. He did the two things he had to do quickly and here am I struggling along. I am getting very cross with myself." He tried again, and again the pot swung in front of him. At the tenth try he managed to climb six feet up the tree, but then the pot swung in front of him and he had to jump off. Angry though he was he would not give up. He began again to climb the tree. Very slowly and carefully he reached a height of ten feet and then the pot began to swing in front of him once more.

Rabbit shouted, "Hang the pot behind you, man. Marmoset, hang the pot behind."

Marmoset had now had enough. "This is the limit," he thought. "Here I am ten feet up a tree with both hands around the trunk, my feet clinging on, the pot swinging about, and Rabbit now tells me to hang the pot behind! How am I supposed to do this? Why didn't Rabbit give this advice before?" Marmoset was so angry that he let the pot swing against the tree while he shouted, "Why didn't you tell me that when I was on the ground?"

The pot swung around, hit the tree, cracked and then broke. A gust of wind blew the sense all over

the world. Some fragments fell on Marmoset and some on Rabbit. Marmoset was still so angry that he shouted, "I'm glad the silly old pot broke."

"Oh! So you are glad, are you?" Gorilla bellowed. First he caught up Rabbit by his pink and white pointed ears, swung him around three times, and threw him across the forest. Each time he swung, Rabbit's ears grew longer: two inches, five inches, six inches. So Rabbit no longer had his small neat ears to match his short tail. Then Gorilla caught Marmoset up by his short tufted tail, swung him around three times and up over the forest. Each time he swung him around, Marmoset's tail grew longer: eight inches, twelve inches, twenty-four inches. And that's why Marmoset has tiny crumpled ears, but a long, long tail.

Gorilla, however, could do nothing about the pot of sense. Sense spread all over the world, and depending on how the wind blew some animals got a lot and some got a little. So . . .

"Wire bend."
And all the animals said,
"Story end."

Big for Me, Little for You

Armadillo moved slowly into the circle of animals to tell his story. He was notorious for moving slowly, so that by the time he was ready Iguana and Firefly were chanting softly, "Break my back, break my back. . . ."

"Shh, shh, have some manners, man," whispered Parrot, while Chimpanzee in a very firm voice said, "Silence, please, silence."

Armadillo did not appear to be in any way put out though, for he began very forcefully,

"Crick Crack."

And they all shouted,

"Break my back."

Armadillo moved right into the story.

The peculiar thing is that although Rabbit had tricked Tiger Cat to get her tears for Gorilla, they remained friends. Perhaps it was because Tiger Cat's mind moved rather slowly. When the earthen pot of sense broke she had been away in her den fast asleep. Bits and pieces of sense fell on Elephant, Dog, Cat, and even on Donkey and most of the other animals, but none fell on Tiger Cat. She was swift like lightning in movement and her claws flashed like steel hooks, but she was really quite a simple animal, relying on her speed and strength.

Though Rabbit had tricked her, she said to herself, "He is a weak, puny individual and will not trick me a second time. He knows that I can nip him to pieces if I want, or take his head off with one bite. He wouldn't dare trick me again."

One morning Rabbit called on Tiger Cat. "Come

fishing with me tomorrow? I have a good line and I am sure Goat will lend you his. It's lots of fun, man, and I think you will like it. There's no hard work involved. All you have to do is sit and let the fish do all the work. They come swimming up, all varieties of them, groupers, speckled sea mullet, striped parrot fish, long-nosed goat fish, yellow-tail snappers. They all swim around the bait, each one greedy for the food. As you sit there you can see them opening and shutting their mouths. Just think of it . . . a yellow-tail snapper sniffs at the bait. Parrot fish thinks he is going to take it and quickly jumps and swallows. Who wins? Why you! All you have to do is pull in the line."

Tiger Cat yawned. "I like meat, red meat and

white meat, any color meat. Rabbit meat is very sweet. If we weren't friends you know what I would have done long ago? A stew, Rabbit, a tasty stew. Oh! I might have even tried you raw."

Rabbit shuddered at the thought, but not too obviously, he hoped. He brought the conversation back to the sea.

"Imagine how nice it will be, Tiger, in the early morning sun. The breeze will be blowing, the sea will be calm. You can just relax on the rock, taking it all in, watching the greedy fish opening and shutting their mouths—fine fish for supper. Fish have lovely white meat too. We are friends, Tiger, and you know friends never eat one another. Will you come fishing?"

"All right, Rabbit, for fish are tasty white meat. When do we start?"

"Early in the morning. I'll knock at your door just before sunrise."

Rabbit did as he had said. He came hopping along, disturbing drops of dew on the grass and navigating through the morning mist.

Down they went to the beach, walking slowly across the white sand, feeling it between their claws. The water was pale green as it slithered silently across the sand. Two dry, dug-out canoes lay on their sides on the beach beside the dark nets hung from bamboo poles to dry. As they walked with their wicker workbaskets and battered tin cans of bait, hermit crabs scattered across the sand.

Rabbit broke the silence. "Soon be sunup time, breakfast time for fish, avocado pear time. Come, Tiger Cat, that is our rock. Let's go."

Rabbit and Tiger Cat sat on the rock and looked into the still green water. Slowly they let down their lines. Tiger Cat said, "Big for me, little for you."

"What did you say, Tiger?"

"Big for me, little for you."

"But, Tiger, be fair. After all I brought you here. We should share what we catch equally."

Tiger drew back her lips a little, just enough for Rabbit to see her razor-sharp teeth. Then she stretched her right foreleg and for one brief moment showed her claws. She repeated very deliberately, "Big for me, little for you."

"Of course, Tiger Cat, of course. Who would think of anything else, much less suggest it." But Rabbit was thinking to himself something else. He was wondering why he had brought Tiger. "I will have to find a way to get my share, a way that does not depend on strength. I will find a way."

The lines hung deep in the water. Bright little fish played in the coral below. A parrot fish came up cautiously, investigating the bait. Suddenly a barracuda sliced in, took the bait and sped out to sea with it. Tiger was so excited she stood there letting

the line run out shouting, "I've got him, I've got a big one!" Rabbit grabbed the line and put Tiger to work. He told her how to play the fish to bring it in. Soon the barracuda lay on the rock beside them, its needle-sharp teeth no longer dangerous.

"It is very fortunate for you that you asked me to come, Rabbit. I am strong and you could never have caught that barracuda yourself. How much do you think it weighs? Must be a twelve-pounder. Such a fight it put up too. It would surely have pulled you into the water, Rabbit. It would have been the fisherman and you the catch. Ah! Big for me, little for you."

Rabbit's nose began to twitch, and soon was quivering so fast he wondered why it did not drop off. He hoped that Tiger would think it was on account of exhaustion. "Think hard, man, think hard. She is all muscle and no brain. Work hard, brains. I must find a way."

The sun crept higher so the red and yellow of the morning sky turned to blue, and clouds began to gather over the hills. The fish stopped biting. It was time to go. Twenty-five fish lay on the rock beside them. Fifteen were large or middle-sized, ten were small, some very small.

Tiger's eyes were bright as she started to do the

sharing. "Big for me, little for you," she chanted,
and into her basket promptly went all the big fish
while into Rabbit's basket she put all the boney
little fish. Tiger's basket was so heavy she found it
hard to lift, but Rabbit had no difficulty in lifting

his. "Yes, little for me this time," Rabbit thought bitterly. Never before had he taken home so much bone and skin for his family.

"What about tomorrow, Tiger. Would you like to go fishing again?"

"I wouldn't miss it for anything. You must appreciate how much luck I have brought to you, Rabbit. Oh, my basket is so heavy I must go inside now. See you, Rabbit."

Rabbit walked home slowly. He put the basket of skin and bone on the table in the kitchen. His wife looked at it and said, "But what bad luck you have had."

"Very bad luck," replied Rabbit. "As you see it's very little for you and the children."

"Yes, that's true, but in this family we share and share alike."

Rabbit sat on the front porch in his rocking chair, rocking and thinking, rocking and thinking. Suddenly he began to smile. He said to himself, "She is quick at running, but I am quicker at thinking. She is quick at starting, but I am quicker at finishing." He called, "Come wife, come children, we have work to do."

When they were all together Rabbit explained his plan very carefully. When he was sure that each knew what he had to do, he mixed some dye. He soon had cans of red, brown, green, purple, yellow, and blue dye. He called the family together again. "Now this plan will not work if you all look the same. Each of you has to be a different color. Then Tiger will not suspect anything." As he spoke he began coloring them. Soon his wife was yellow, his eldest son blue, and the other little rabbits were purple, red, brown, and green.

Next morning, just before sunup, Rabbit knocked at Tiger Cat's gate. Off they set. Tiger was in a good mood. She chatted on and on about the wonderful stew her mother had made and what a lovely barracuda breakfast she had just eaten. "This morning I will bring you luck again like I did yesterday."

As soon as they had settled themselves on the rocks and let down their lines the fish began biting. Each time Rabbit caught a big fish Tiger sang, "Big for me, little for you," and each time Tiger caught a little fish he sang, "Little for you, big for me."

When they were finished fishing Tiger shared the catch between them. This time she had caught only small fish, but this did not prevent her from singing loudly, "Big for me, little for you."

Tiger could hardly lift her heavy basket, while Rabbit slung his easily over one arm. About halfway back to Tiger's house Rabbit sat down under a tree breathing heavily. "I'm not feeling so well, Tiger Cat, but you had better hurry on, because your fish might spoil in the sun."

"I would wait with you, Rabbit, but you are quite right. All these beautiful fish might spoil. See you in the morning."

Tiger rounded the first corner and came upon a small red rabbit, lying flat on its back with its legs stuck up in the air. "A dead red rabbit," she muttered and moved on. Round the next corner she saw a small brown rabbit lying in the middle of the road with its legs up in the air. "A dead brown rabbit," she muttered to herself. A little farther on she saw a blue rabbit also lying in the middle of the road. "A dead blue rabbit," she muttered. Fifty yards farther she saw a large yellow rabbit in a position similar to the others. "A dead yellow rabbit," she muttered. Just beyond the yellow rabbit Tiger found a purple rabbit, quite small, flat on its back in the middle of the road, its legs stiff in the air. "A dead purple rabbit," she muttered. Some yards ahead she passed a dead green rabbit. "A dead green rabbit," she muttered to herself.

Suddenly she stopped, put down the basket of fish and cried out. "How very stupid. I have passed six rabbits. I have passed a dead red rabbit, a dead green rabbit, a dead purple rabbit, a dead blue rabbit, a brown one, and a yellow one. If they were all brown rabbits I might think Rabbit was up to his tricks. But I can tell from the colors that these are not all from the same family. Six rabbits!" She counted on her claws. "I must run

back and get them. What a feast!" Tiger put down
the basket and sped off down the road looking for
the rabbits.

Meanwhile Rabbit, who had waited until Tiger
was out of sight, ran to join the little green rabbit. Quickly his wife and all the other little rabbits
came hopping and jumping through the bushes.
They were very quiet so that Tiger wouldn't hear
them. All the rabbits took turns carrying the
heavy basket of fish. They were happy. Now they
had enough fish for a whole week.

The following morning Rabbit woke up smiling. He whispered to himself, "All for me, none for you."

So,

"Wire bend."

And the animals replied,

"Story end."

Everyone was laughing, everyone that is except Hacka Tiger. He was very quiet. Only the tip of his tail twitched slightly. He got up slowly and moved silently into the darkness. "Why did they always have to make tigers look foolish in their stories. Did they really think that tigers had no sense at all, that a weak, little floppity-eared creature like Rabbit could get the better of a big, strong tiger?"

Forty Men I See,
Forty Men I Do Not See

Dusk had crept over the forest as the animals gathered for Parrot's story. As they settled down, chatting while they made themselves comfortable, Owl looked around the group from her perch. She noticed that Hacka Tiger was sulking. His face was long and he sat far apart from the group, watching, but not sharing in any of the fun.

Just before Parrot moved into the center of the circle, Capuchin jumped up with two small stones, one in each hand. He struck them together sharply so that they made a noise that sounded like crick crack.

The animals laughed, all except Hacka Tiger

who growled, "Capuchin, you are always thinking up tricks, but Parrot, you must still say the words."

Parrot screeched,

"Crick Crack."

And all the animals replied,

"Break my back."

One day Old Woman Crim decided to give a party. She is the witch woman who lived in the dry forest that used to be our old home. Her hut was in the shadow of the craggy limestone rocks high above the cool, comforting trees. The rocks were rough, bald, and bleak, not covered in cool moss like those below. Only a scraggly patch of grass grew and here and there some skeleton cactus. No one but Mother Crim and her companion Dry Bones liked the place. But then, she even looked like the rocks. Her face was craggy, with tufts of long stiff hairs; her nose was sharp like a broken rock and her mouth was thin and tight. Even when she was happy only the corners of her mouth stretched a bit. Her laugh was like a dry high screech.

Old Woman Crim gave good parties and whenever she invited the animals they went. They were afraid to go, but they were more afraid not to go.

Old Woman Crim screeched to Dry Bones early one morning, "Dry Bones, Dry Bones, let's have a party for the animals on Monday evening. Go and invite everyone—that is, everyone except Rabbit. Rabbit must not come!"

Dry Bones cackled. He was always helping Old Woman Crim. Sometimes he gathered the herbs for her magic. His name was just right for him. He was boney looking, with a thin, leathery, scaly skin stretched over his skull and shoulder blades and over his ribs and legs. Even his voice was dry. It sounded like brown leaves blowing in the wind. He could walk for miles, searching for dead toads, lizards' tails, and other specialties for Old Woman Crim's brews.

For several years in a row now Old Woman Crim had given extravagant parties, always with some mischief in mind. But each time the animals had gone home safely after the party. When Old Woman Crim whispered her latest plans to Dry Bones, though, he really cackled and rubbed his dry hands together. This time it would be different. It would be a very special party.

Off rattled Dry Bones to invite Dog, Goat, Cat, Mongoose, and all the animals he met on the way. At the little post office he put up a big sign with the names of all those who were to be invited to the party.

"Old Woman Crim might be an old witch woman," said Dog, "but she knows how to give a party. She has good music and, best of all, lots to eat. I

must admit I like to eat. I think I'll skip lunch that day so that I have an extra good appetite for dinner."

"Me too," said Cat, who was currently on speaking terms with Dog.

"Last year there was a lot of good food, but remember the party had a bad ending. It's rather strange that she hasn't invited Rabbit this time. I wonder why?"

Rabbit also wondered why he had not been invited. He remembered the year before. At that party Screech Owl had come with White Rooster, and when White Rooster crowed to say it was daylight, Owl had flown away before Old Woman Crim could catch her. Rabbit remembered how much this had pleased him, how he had laughed, hopping up and down crying, "You won't catch Owl, Old Woman Crim, not a chance." He also recalled his warning to her. "From now on I'll be watching for your tricks, and you too, Dry Bones. I'll never stop watching you."

"Aha!" Rabbit thought. "I bet they are up to something again so they do not want me there. That's why I haven't been asked. Well, this means that I shall have to watch them even more closely, for they must be planning something evil. What I'll do is pretend to go and visit my cousin over the hill and keep a very bright eye on Old Woman Crim and Dry Bones."

Monday evening came and Old Woman Crim waited for her guests. She welcomed them and led them to the table which held large dishes of lovely food. There was so much food the animals had difficulty in choosing what to start with. "Whatever else one might say, Old Woman Crim knows how to give a party," they all agreed.

They began to eat, quickly at first and then more slowly, hoping that if they ate slowly they could hold more food.

Meanwhile, outside the kitchen window Rabbit was hiding. Dry Bones was very busy. He had four big pots on the stove and kept adding wood to the fire. Rabbit managed to peep through the window and saw that the pots had only water in them. Now he was really curious. As he strained to see, he heard Dry Bones singing in a reedy voice,

> *"Forty men I see,*
> *Forty men I do not see*
> *In the valley.*
> *Forty men I see,*
> *Forty men I do not see*
> *In the valley."*

Rabbit was becoming quite worried now, for he saw no food going into the pots. Dry Bones stirred, sang, and glanced at the door with a wicked grin.

Rabbit was puzzled. What could this mean? There was a great deal of food in the other room. All the animals were eating and drinking. Why did

Dry Bones have the pots on the stove with nothing cooking in them? Why was Dry Bones singing,

> *"Forty men I see,*
> *Forty men I do not see. . . ."?*

Suddenly Rabbit wondered, "How many animals are in the room?"

Rabbit crept around to the front of the house, where he came upon Dog.

Poor Dog had eaten too much and had come outside to sit in the cool and recover. His stomach was so full, the room so hot, the animals so loud that he just had to have some air. When Dog saw Rabbit he was startled but managed to silence his bark when he heard Rabbit's whisper.

"You are all in danger. Quickly but quietly, go and count how many animals are in the room and come and tell me. Don't let anyone realize what you are doing though."

Dog crept back into the room. Pretending to be casually walking around, he counted, then he went back to the doorway and whispered, "Thirty-nine animals, but counting me that's forty."

"Just as I thought," said Rabbit. "Now I know what Dry Bones' song means.

> 'Forty men I see
> Forty men I do not see.'

"Dog, you must do what I tell you. Go to the kitchen door, peep inside, and if you see Dry Bones with four large pots of boiling water on the stove, give the alarm. All of you must run to the river as quickly as possible. I will have a boat waiting for you."

Dog was very frightened, but he tried to act brave and not show how frightened he was. He drifted back into the room, slowly opened the door, and through the steam he saw Dry Bones stirring and singing,

> "Forty men I do not see."

Dog's nose began to sweat. He hurried back into the room and barked sharply. "Danger, danger. Follow me. Run as fast as you can. Run for your lives. Follow me."

As Dog set off the other animals followed. Cat dropped the piece of fish she had been chewing. Duck swallowed his corn pone, as they all tumbled through the doorway. Goat was so busy munching that he didn't realize what was happening until the other animals were almost through the door.

Rabbit was waiting with a boat, and as they rowed across the river he explained what had happened. All of them got safely across, all except Goat

who arrived after the boat had left. Goat could not swim. He ran up and down the beach looking for somewhere to hide. His only chance was to bury himself in the sand. He quickly dug a hole, and hid himself in it, but he did not realize that his horns were sticking out like two small dry wooden stumps.

By the time Dry Bones had rattled down to the river the animals had escaped. He was extremely

angry. He ran up and down the beach searching for something to throw at the animals. As he ran he stubbed his toe on two dry stumps sticking out of the sand.

"Ah!" he cried, "these will be just right to throw at those wretched animals, and I hope I hit that Rabbit."

He bent down creakily, gathered all his strength together, pulled on the stumps and threw them across the river. When he saw that he had thrown Goat, he was very angry. "If only I had known,

I could still have had some good curry." He rattled his way back up to Old Woman Crim. They
would have to plan again, for Rabbit had spoiled
their party after all.

"Wire bend."
And all the animals joined in, saying,
"Story end."

Riddle Me Riddle,
Riddle Me Ree

Chimpanzee sat with his head buried deep in his chest. He was going over all the riddles he knew. He wanted to find the three best ones. So far all had gone well. Hacka Tiger, though he had sulked occasionally, had not tried to carry Iguana off, and Capuchin had played only one trick. Best of all Chimpanzee had enjoyed the food the animals had brought. His mouth began to water as he remembered the delicious guava tart that Armadillo had shared with him the night before.

There was a rustling in the leaves. "Here comes Capuchin," thought Chimpanzee, "but he's not chattering away as he usually does. Something must have happened."

Capuchin swung swiftly down from the branch of a tree and sprang to Chimpanzee's side. He whispered in Chimpanzee's ear. "Man-with-a-Gun is on the farside of the forest, the side where the sun dips down."

"Where do you mean? Is he by the creek that runs into the big river?"

"Right there. I hid and watched him for a while. I believe he has come to stay, for he is clearing land and he's brought Woman with him. I believe he has come to stay, for he would not go to all that trouble if he were *not* going to stay. I smell danger ahead, Chimpanzee."

Chimpanzee thought quickly and quietly. Capuchin was right. This could mean trouble. The animals would have to avoid that area; they would have to move more carefully around the forest. "Tomorrow I will check on it, but let's not say anything until we are sure. We will go and investigate and then discuss with Owl what we should do."

As he finished speaking they could hear Green Parrot announcing her presence with loud squawks. The other animals began to arrive, chattering and laughing as they usually did over the stories they had heard.

Chimpanzee demanded silence. He said, "I have my three riddles ready. Do you have your food ready?" Parrot glanced at Iguana and winked. They had been laughing about Chimpanzee's immense appetite. Chimpanzee continued. "Here is riddle number four.

> *Riddle me riddle, riddle me ree,*
> *Guess me this riddle and perhaps not.*
> *My father has a cock.*
> *Everytime it crows, it crows fire."*

Everyone was quiet. Only the evening breeze could be heard moving gently through the trees. Firefly closed his eyes, Hacka Tiger furrowed his brow, Brown Owl spread her wings and then folded them. In the back of Hacka Tiger's mind a memory stirred. A crow meant a noise. Crowing fire— that must be something that makes a noise with fire and smoke.

The dim memory stirred again. It was becoming sharper. He felt cold with an old fear. He saw his mother running with him to the bushes to escape a sharp sound and a sudden flash. "Man-with-a-Gun, that's what it was!" he thought to himself.

"Man-with-a-Gun," he roared.

"Correct," said Chimpanzee. "Tomorrow night we will hear the story you want to tell us."

Armadillo said, "That was not a nice riddle, Chimpanzee, but at least we don't have to worry about 'Man-with-a-Gun' here."

Chimpanzee began with the fifth riddle immediately. He was not going to give Capuchin a chance to let their secret slip out.

> *"Riddle me riddle, riddle me ree,*
> *Guess me this riddle and perhaps not.*
> *John Redman tickles John Blackman*
> *Until he sings.*
> *He whistles and sings.*
> *Guess me this riddle."*

Almost before he had finished Iguana called out "A pot on the fire. I know another story about Dry Bones and pots."

"Just a minute, Iguana. You are right, but don't start the story now. You have to wait your turn," Chimpanzee said, calling her to order. "Now here is the final riddle.

Riddle me riddle, riddle me ree,
Guess me this riddle and perhaps not.
My father was riding at full speed,
Riding high, riding at full speed.
His hat fell off.
He never stopped to pick it up."

Parrot objected loudly. "That's too hard. It's not a proper riddle. I don't see how anyone could guess that riddle."

Firefly flashed his light and agreed. "I can't even begin to think of the answer to that one."

"It is a proper riddle. I am the chairman and if I say so, it is so," Chimpanzee ruled. "Who is going to guess this one?"

Firefly looked up at the sky and saw a falling star. "A falling star," he said. "A falling star rides fast and high!"

"That is not right. Just stop and think!" Chimpanzee commanded.

Brown Owl muttered, "Well, if it's not a star, something else that rides fast and high is a bird."

Parrot objected. "We birds don't wear hats! That's a more foolish answer than Firefly's was."

"But," Brown Owl replied, "when a feather falls from a bird he does not stop to pick it up."

"All right, all right! Brown Owl is right. She will tell the final story. Now it's food time. Let the sharing begin," Chimpanzee said eagerly.

Early the next morning Chimpanzee and Capuchin set off to investigate the Man-with-a-Gun. They traveled away from the rising sun, and they were careful not to leave the parts of the forest where the trees grow tall and close together. They would take no chances, even though it was early in the day. Finally the trees thinned out and they could hear the brown water flowing in the creek. They peeped out from behind some bushes, heard a rustling and crunching of pebbles, then they saw the man. He was carrying a gun and a dead wild turkey as he walked towards a small shack.

"It *is* a man, and he does seem to be going to settle here. He is out early," whispered Chimpanzee. "We must tell Owl. Perhaps the forest is big

enough for all of us. I hope so. We should not have
to move. I hope there is enough space for all of us."

Horns for a Rabbit

That night, when all the animals had gathered for the party, Hacka Tiger sprang into the center of the circle. He had his story all ready. He was tired of tales in which little Rabbit made Tiger look foolish. He would tell them a story in which Rabbit gets a comeuppance. He growled,
"Crick Crack."
The animals jumped, but replied,
"Break my back!"

Long ago my cousin Tiger Cat lived alone on an island. It was a special island for it was not in the sea, but in the middle of a river, a river so big that it was almost a sea. This island was a very safe place to live, for no Man-with-a-Gun ever went there, but like most safe places it was lonely. Every month Tiger Cat gave a party at full moon. This gave her a chance to be with the other animals and because the moon was full and bright they had a chance to get home safely after the party.

As usual the animals got quite excited as the time for Tiger's party came closer. They enjoyed parties. This time, however, many of the animals were disappointed. For some reason Tiger had invited only the animals with horns. Duck, Tiger's boatman, was not going to allow any animal into the boat who did not have horns.

This pleased the animals with horns greatly. Goat ran through the village shouting, "Look at my horns. These horns are my tickets to Tiger's party!" In front of Dog's house he stopped and called in a loud voice, "Look at my horns. Wouldn't you love a pair of horns like this, Dog? Maybe the blacksmith could make you a pair. Ha! I have my horns already made."

The animals without horns were angry. Dog and Rabbit were especially angry. They had never missed one of Tiger's parties before. They discussed it together. Dog told how Goat had come taunting him and asking him why he didn't get the blacksmith to make him a pair of horns. Rabbit's brain began to turn over. "But that's a good idea, Dog."

"What? What is a good idea?"

"To get the blacksmith to fit us out with horns. He has in his shop the horns of his favorite goats, the two that died last year."

"Yes, I know, but what good is that to us? How could he fit them on our heads? What do you think he could do with your ears, anyway?"

"Let's try," said Rabbit. "I want to go to the party. Maybe he can arrange the horns so that they hide my ears."

The blacksmith listened to them, measured their heads and then measured the horns. "I don't really want to use these horns. They are all I have left of my two lovely goats, and I would not want anything to happen to them." He tried the larger

pair on Dog and the smaller pair on Rabbit. The blacksmith looked very thoughtful. "Dog, I think I can make you look quite good, but Rabbit, it will be more difficult with you. Those long ears of yours get in the way and the horns are quite heavy you know."

"It's all right, man. They may be heavy, but I won't have to wear them for very long. Once the party has started I can take them off and I'm sure no one will notice."

"I will try!" replied the blacksmith. "I can do Dog's quickly and will work on yours after."

The blacksmith began to work on Dog's horns. He tried to work quickly for there was little time. Rabbit was watching impatiently. "Is that comfortable? Is it comfortable now?" he kept asking Dog. Dog would continue telling the blacksmith where they hurt the most. The blacksmith sawed away while Rabbit jumped around the shop. "Hurry, hurry up, you have to do mine too, you know."

Finally the blacksmith was finished with Dog. Dog felt very smart. The horns fitted comfortably and were held to his head by a thin strap of the same color as his skin and hair.

"Don't they just suit me, Rabbit?"

"They look like horns," Rabbit answered impatiently. "You've got your party tickets now, but what about me? And it was my idea. I do not want to be left here alone, while you go off with Goat to the party."

Dog was feeling very frisky. "The idea was really Goat's, but I'll wait for you. I'll just practice a few jumps while I wait." Dog began to jump about, but suddenly he stopped. "No! The strap might work loose. I'd better be careful. I will wait for you as long as I can."

The blacksmith began to work on Rabbit's horns. It was a difficult job. Rabbit's head was small and his ears were big. When it was almost time for the boat to leave the blacksmith was still sawing and chopping. They were almost right, but not quite. Dog became quite anxious. He did not want to leave Rabbit, but even more than that he did not want to miss the party.

"Rabbit," he said, "the boat will go in a little while. I'll walk to the pier now and try to persuade Duck and Tiger to wait for you."

Off went Dog. He walked very carefully so that his strap would not slip off. The boat was ready to leave, and instead of asking Duck to wait, he slipped on board, anxious not to attract any attention in case he was recognized.

With five minutes to go before the boat was due to leave, Rabbit was desperate. The horns were still too heavy. Rabbit knew they would never fit comfortably. They would always be too heavy for him. He rushed from the blacksmith's shop and arrived at the pier just in time to see the boat being pushed off.

Rabbit could see Dog standing among the horned animals. He began to stamp his feet. "It is just not fair," he muttered. "Those stupid animals are going to the party because they have horns while I, Rabbit, cleverest of them all, the one to whom they all come for advice, am left standing on the pier."

He began to shout and shriek as loud as he could. "Captain Tiger Cat, Boatman Duck, test the horns."

Tiger Cat could not hear very well because she was rowing. She stopped, leaned on the oars, and asked, "Who is calling me? Have we left someone behind?"

Dog shouted quickly, "No, no one is left. Rabbit says you are to row fast. A squall is blowing up."

"Did he say that?" Goat asked, somewhat puzzled. "It is Rabbit, but I thought he said something about tapping horns. Wait, he's calling again."

Dog hurriedly said, "It sounds as if he's saying 'Have a good time, have a good time!'"

"No," said Tiger Cat, "that was not what I heard. The wind blew some of the words away, but I heard something about tapping Dog's horns. I don't understand that, because there is no dog on board."

Duck looked around at the animals in the boat. She looked at their heads and then at their feet. "If those aren't Dog's feet, then mine are not webbed," she thought. Looking at Tiger Cat she said, "Why not do what Rabbit says? We do not know why he says it, but he usually has a reason."

"Tap horns," Tiger Cat commanded.

Duck watched Dog. She saw that Dog did not laugh or tap his horns sharply like the others did.

Once more Rabbit's words came drifting over the water. "You have Dog on board. Tap his horns, tap his horns."

Duck took up a little wooden hammer. "If Dog is on board we shall soon know." She began to tap the horns of the animals. She tapped the horns of Little Deer who was sitting next to Dog. Then she tapped Dog's horns sharply and they shifted to one side.

"It's Dog, it's Dog," shouted Duck. But before she could say anything else Dog had jumped overboard and was swimming swiftly to the bank. Rabbit, however, did not stand and watch his arrival. He began to run at full speed for his home. Dog followed close behind, but Rabbit dived into his hole.

Now you know why Rabbit always runs away when he sees Dog. So,

"Wire bend."

And all the animals said,

"Story end."

After supper, just before the animals began to go home, Chimpanzee called them to order again.

"I have something to tell you. Man-with-a-Gun is here. Capuchin and I saw him this morning. He is on the farside of the forest, to the west. I think it would be wise if we kept away from that part of the forest. The trouble is that Man is always so ready to kill. We stay away from him but he hunts us down. He won't let us share the forest with him in peace. But for the present Owl and I think there is no need to worry. Soon Capuchin and I will make another journey to check on what Man is doing. We hope the forest can hold all of us."

Lizard and a Ring of Gold

The animals came quietly to Chimpanzee's house on the night Iguana was to tell her story. Iguana and Firefly were early. They wanted to know if Owl had planned anything for them to do about the Man-with-a-Gun. Green Parrot was also early. She had not slept well at all. It seemed that every time the cock crowed it crowed fire. How she wished that she had never heard that riddle! She too was anxious to hear Owl's plan.

Most of the animals had gathered before Capuchin and Chimpanzee arrived. Owl flew in with them, her wings flapping like loose sails in the dim light of the forest. To the west hung a black thunder cloud, its ragged edges torn apart now and then by lightning. The sky overhead was still clear as Iguana looked up to see the first stars twinkling. "I do like it here," she said to Firefly.

Firefly answered by turning on his headlamps for a moment and making clicking sounds. "Yes, I think we will be able to stay," he said. "Chimpanzee is even smiling. Owl and Capuchin look satisfied. I think it will be all right."

"But, what a lot you saw in that little time," Iguana replied.

"I can't keep my headlamps on for long," explained Firefly. "They flash on and off, on and off, so I have had to learn to see things quickly. I see everything in a flash."

Chimpanzee quickly called the meeting to order. "Iguana is going to tell the story this evening, but before she begins, let me tell you our plan for the Man-with-a-Gun. We, Capuchin and I, have spent the day watching him. The young ones are scratching at the surface of the earth and scattering seeds. They are no danger to us."

"They might not be," said Hacka Tiger, "but the man still has a gun and that is a danger to us."

"We realize that, Hacka Tiger, so we stopped on the way and talked with Brown Owl. She has a plan. Tell us what it is, Owl."

Brown Owl flew into the center of the circle and blinked twice before speaking.

"We must watch Man carefully. We are quite safe while he plants, reaps, and builds, but we are in danger when he leaves his home to come into the forest, our home, with a gun. We must watch him, so that we know what he is doing at all times."

"How can we do that?" squawked Parrot. "Even if we took turns it would be difficult. We have to watch from far off. We cannot go into his house. And we would get tired of watching day after day and week after week."

"None of us will have to spend our time watching, for we already have three watchmen," Brown Owl answered.

"Who are they?" asked Firefly. "Not Dog, for he is with Man, and not Horse, for Horse is also with Man. They won't watch for us."

"This is also true of Cow," Brown Owl said, "but we have three fine watchmen. One is White Heron who always stays near Man's cows, feeding off the insects in the pasture. The second is Spider Man who lives inside Man's house and the third is Lizard who is always going in and out of Man's house.

Hacka Tiger looked a little anxious and he asked, "When you speak of the Spider Man, do you mean Anansi?"

"I do mean Anansi," Brown Owl replied. "I know that he is full of tricks and might try to mislead us if he thought he could gain by doing so. However, we can check his reports with those from White Heron and Lizard."

Chimpanzee joined in. "Yes, I don't really trust Anansi either, but he *is* in Man's house all the time. We have all three so that's a good warning system. At least one of them will know when Man is going hunting, and Lizard, White Heron, and Anansi are not friends, so they won't join together to put us in the power of Man-with-a-Gun."

Hacka Tiger still looked upset, but he could not think of a better plan, so he snarled, "We can try and see how it works, but don't say I didn't warn you. Now, let's get on with the story. It's getting quite late. Iguana, are you ready?"

"Yes," answered Iguana, "and in my story I will tell you why it is that White Heron, Anansi, and Lizard keep out of each other's way. This is an Anansi story so we won't begin with the words 'Crick Crack.'

"We'll begin,

Once upon a time and a long, long time ago when the world and time were young, Anansi, White Heron, and Lizard were firm friends. They lived close together and were always ready to help each other. They worked together, planting, weeding, and reaping and they shared whatever they had.

In those days Woodpecker was a great traveler. He was the one who brought news to all the villages. One day he came with special news, news which made them all very excited. The King had promised that anyone who could make his daughter laugh, or even smile, would be given one of her gold rings. Woodpecker explained to them that she was a very sad girl, who had never been known to laugh. "Why don't you try, Anansi? Think of it, if you only made her smile, even a little smile, you would get the ring, and think of all the food and fine clothes the King might also give you!"

Anansi did not waste any time. Quickly he got together a band of musicians. Cricket would play the castanets. Frog would beat the big bass drum, and Mockingbird would play the violin. They set off for the Palace. As they marched along other animals joined in, making it a little procession. There was Donkey kicking his heels in the air as he danced, Horse tapping out the music, and Cow tossing her tail and her horns and singing the only note she knew, "Moo-moo-moo."

The Palace gates opened, and they all marched through. People came running to look. At the sight of Donkey dancing, Frog playing music, and Cow singing, the King laughed and the Queen laughed, but the girl was sad. Her eyes neither smiled nor laughed. The animals looked at her and one by one they became silent. Cricket and Mockingbird stopped playing and Frog stopped beating the drum.

They all became sad and quiet, just like the girl. Anansi turned around and led his gloomy band out of the Palace yard.

Next, White Heron decided that he would try to make the girl laugh. Now, White Heron is a fairly large bird with an elegant head on a long, slender neck, and sticklike black legs. He thought to himself, "Perhaps Old Woman Crim will help me. I often help her by eating the ticks on her cow. She will help me to find some way of making the girl laugh."

Old Woman Crim agreed to help White Heron. They thought out a secret plan. She gave him a hat, umbrella, jacket, shirt, tie, socks, shoes, and, best of all, a pair of long flannel trousers that suited his coloring.

Lizard, who had been watching the fitting, asked Old Woman Crim, "How will White Heron ever take off these clothes? He could not have put them on without your help and if you aren't there, he'll never get them off."

Old Woman Crim replied, "That is no problem, for these are special clothes. If White Heron sings this song, the clothes will fall off by themselves."

She sang:

> *"Quasheeba, Quasheeba*
> *And now you must go*
> *From head down to toe*
> *Cantinny Quasheeba*
> *From hat down to shoe*
> *Quasheeba calls you*
> *Cantinny Quasheeba*
> *Strips you."*

White Heron walked proudly. He thought how smart he looked and held his neck even straighter than before. The Palace gates opened immediately, for the gatekeepers had seen him coming. The King came into the courtyard to admire the man who looked so elegantly dressed. Lizard felt very dull beside White Heron.

It was not polite, but the King could not help laughing at this dressed-up stranger with a long, thin neck and very long, thin legs. The Queen

laughed too, and called her daughter, who stepped
into the courtyard. She slowly lifted her eyes to look
at White Heron, but they remained sad. When the
King and Queen saw that she had not smiled they
stopped laughing. White Heron did not know what

to do, and his own happiness fell away from him. Lizard, who had been feeling somewhat envious of all the attention White Heron was getting, perked up. He looked at the King cheekily and said, "I will make your daughter laugh." He turned toward the daughter and began to sing:

> "Quasheeba, Quasheeba
> And now you must go
> From head down to toe
> Cantinny Quasheeba
> From hat down to shoe
> Quasheeba calls you
> Cantinny Quasheeba
> Strips you."

As Lizard sang White Heron's hat flew straight up into the air. The umbrella with the gold handle flew from White Heron's hand. Then the jacket flew off Heron's back, followed by his shirt and tie. The fine flannel trousers fell from his long black legs and the socks and shoes flew from his feet. How funny it was to see the clothes flying in all directions!

Everyone stared at Heron in amazement. They even forgot to watch the girl to see if she were laughing. They would have been surprised, for as she watched, her eyes brightened, her mouth

twitched slightly, and then a smile spread over her
face till even her eyes were alive. She began to
laugh and her laughter rang out like a little silver
bell, clear and happy.

The King and Queen began to dance with joy,
and when he could speak again, the King called to

Lizard, "You have won the golden ring!" As he spoke he threw it to Lizard.

White Heron was angry, for he felt he should have the ring. After all, it was he whom everyone had laughed at. With his beak he tried to get the ring away from Lizard. To protect the ring Lizard put it in his mouth and in all the excitement he swallowed it. The ring stuck in his throat and has stayed there to this day. Sometimes you can see him blowing air into the skin under his throat, and the skin is bright orange and gold, for it takes on the color of the ring.

Lizard, White Heron, and Anansi never again became friends, for each felt that the other two had tried to outdo him. They all go their own ways now, White Heron in the pasture on his long black legs, Anansi high in the corner of a room where he spins his web, and Lizard, croaking and moving his head up and down as he crawls along the ground.

The Grass-Cutting Races

"This is the last evening of our party," Capuchin said softly to Tiger, stroking the black hair on the back of his head. "When Brown Owl suggested a party that would last a week and a day it seemed like a long time, but it is almost over already."

Hacka Tiger said, "Yes, the time has gone quickly. We have come to the end of the party." Now that they all had to be on guard against Man, the other animals felt more kindly toward Hacka Tiger. Tiger had even made friends with Iguana—for the time being at least.

Even Chimpanzee, as he sat thinking about Man and his family, said, "This party was a good idea of mine." Then, remembering Parrot, he added quickly, "And Parrot's too. I am sorry that to-night is the last night. I have enjoyed the stories and of course the food." Chimpanzee had spent the morning watching Man and his family. The Man's young ones had been fishing in the dark creek water. Woman was cooking while Man turned over heavy clods of moist earth.

The animals were all anxious for the evening's party to begin and to have it last as long as possible. Chimpanzee opened the party, saying, "After Brown Owl has told her story we will have supper. It has been a good party and I do not think we need fear Man-with-a-Gun. I have been watching him. He is getting his land ready for planting. If we keep to this side of the forest and let him have his side we should be all right. If at any time we appear to be in danger, I will call another meeting. Now, Brown Owl, are you ready with your story?"

Brown Owl flew into the middle of the circle. "Anansi is going to watch Man for us, but we must watch him, for he is always playing tricks. Sometimes he takes the shape of a spider in a web and at other times he is a man, a man with a very quick mind and a very large appetite. When you hear my story of how he tricked Old Woman Crim and Dry Bones you'll see why we must watch our watchman Anansi.

Once upon a time and a long, long time ago it was, Old Woman Crim lived in a dry and craggy area. She had managed, however, to grow two patches of green guinea grass for her cows to eat. But in the larger field along with the grass grew nettles, horrible stinging nettles called cow-itch and how they could itch. If a leaf lightly touched you, it felt as if you were on fire and you had to scratch and scratch.

One morning Old Woman Crim put on her "get-ready" voice and called loudly to Dry Bones. "Time to get those fields of grass cut," she said.

Dry Bones echoed her, "Time to get those fields of grass cut."

Old Woman Crim laughed. "How those animals will itch, how they will scratch. Oh! It will do me good to see Goat, Monkey, Anansi, and the others itching and scratching. How I will laugh."

"Why will they itch?" Dry Bones asked. "What is going to get them into the fields to cut grass?"

"We will have two races," she replied. "Whoever cuts the grass in the large field without scratching himself once will win a calf. How I will laugh at them, itching and scratching, scratching and itching. I will not have to give away the calf. I can offer the prize because I know they can't win.

"In the small field whoever cuts the most grass will get a chicken. It will be one of my oldest, scrawniest chickens, but no one will know how poor a prize it is until both my fields are cut. Now go and tell Parrot about the races. She loves to talk. She will be sure to pass on the news to everyone."

"To make absolutely certain I will tell Woodpecker too, for whatever he hears he tells," Dry Bones said, laughing.

Parrot and Woodpecker did tell everyone, for on Monday morning when Old Woman Crim and Dry Bones looked out at the fields they saw them full of hopeful animals. Some, like Parrot and Wood-pecker, were there to watch. Goat, Monkey, Dog, Anansi, and many others were there to win the calf or the chicken.

"First of all," shrieked Old Woman Crim, "you must cut the large field, the field with the cow-itch, and remember that whoever scratches is out of the race. Dry Bones will watch you. All those ready to start line up here!"

The animals lined up, holding their sharp grass knives tightly. Dry Bones crackled, "Away you go!" and Old Woman Crim echoed, "Away you go." Then she added softly, "And scratch and scratch and scratch and scratch."

As they set off, a patch of cow-itch caught Mon-key's right foot. He dropped the grass knife and with both hands he scratched his foot, howling with agony. Dry Bones did not have to tell him to fall out of the race. Monkey leaped across the fence, ran at full speed to the stream and plunged in, desperately trying to put out the fire that raged on his foot.

Old Woman Crim shrieked with laughter, mock-

ing him, calling after him, "What happened to you, Monkey? Aren't you going to try for the calf, Monkey, the fat, fat calf?"

Anansi was working down the middle of the large field. The cow-itch nipped his left leg, near the ankle. He stopped. Dry Bones was watching him. Anansi could hardly speak, so strong was the wish to scratch and scratch. "Look, Dry Bones," said Anansi, "there's a centipede on your leg, just here, just here." He bent down and scratched his

leg where the cow-itch had stung him, calling out to
Dry Bones, "A centipede, here on your ankle, Dry
Bones."

Dry Bones stooped down to look for the centipede, but could not find it.

Anansi called out, "You're lucky, Dry Bones,
it's gone, it's gone."

Five yards farther on, a patch of cow-itch stung
Anansi on the right arm, below the elbow. "Fire!" he
thought. "My skin is on fire!" He knew he just had

to scratch. "Look, Dry Bones, a mosquito on your right arm, just here, just here!" He rubbed and scratched his right arm below the elbow, calling directions to Dry Bones, telling him where the mosquito was.

"Ah, Dry Bones," he said, "that kind of mosquito can make you ill. I am glad it has gone."

By this time Dog and Goat had joined Monkey in the cool stream, their skin burning with the cow-itch. Old Woman Crim cackled and hooted with pleasure as she watched them. Only Anansi kept cutting the grass. As he drew near to the end of the field a large patch of cow-itch caught him on both hands. "Fire! Fire!" he thought.

"Dry Bones," he said, "when you are very cold do you rub your hands together like this?" and he rubbed his two burning hands together to soothe them. "Like this, Dry Bones?" he asked. "When it's cold at night, do you rub them together like this?"

"Exactly like that, Anansi, exactly like that," Dry Bones replied. "I hate the cold so I spend most of the time rubbing my hands together."

"Well," shouted Anansi, as he finished and jumped out of the field, "I have won the calf, Dry Bones. Let's go and get it."

"Did you see him scratch?" asked Old Woman Crim.

"No, he never scratched himself, not once," said Dry Bones. "I know he is clever so I watched him all the time. He didn't scratch once. And you will have to give him the calf, Old Woman Crim, for everybody knows you promised it."

"I've taken my calf home," said Anansi. "Now let's get on with the second race! Who is in the race?"

Ten animals entered for the grass-cutting race in the small field. There was no cow-itch in that field, but the grass was long and tough. Monkey, the champion grass cutter, was there. So were Tiger, Goat, Dog, and others.

"Ready!" called Dry Bones.

"Wait a moment," shrieked Old Woman Crim. She was very angry at having to give away the calf, and it was too late now to cancel the second race. But she would keep a sharp lookout to see that no one played tricks on her. She said, "Parrot and Woodpecker will fly overhead and watch the race. Show me your grass knives." Old Woman Crim inspected the grass knives. They were all the same size.

"Show me your bags." She inspected the bags into which the animals were to put the grass they cut. They were all empty. "Start them off, Dry Bones!" she called.

"Ready!" called Dry Bones.

"Steady!"

"Go!"

The air was full of the swishing sound of grass
being cut. It was hard work. The sun was high in
the sky, the air was hot, the stalks of guinea grass
were thick as pencils and tough, and the long
blades of grass had edges sharp as knives. Monkey
was soon bleeding from cuts on his skin. He moved
quickly and therefore was not as careful as he
should have been. He carried a gourd of cool water
strapped around his waist. Dog carried a bottle of
water slung over his shoulder. Anansi had not
brought any water with him. He cut as fast as he

could, but his bag was only one-sixth full when Monkey's was one-quarter full. Rooster shouted, "Stick to it, Anansi, stick to it."

Tiger Cat called out, "You're ahead, Monkey! You're well ahead, Monkey, you're well ahead!"

The ten animals bent to the work. Parrot squawked overhead. Woodpecker broadcast news of the race, saying, "Monkey's bag is half full, Dog's bag is one-quarter full, Anansi's bag is one-quarter full . . ." and so on.

Anansi moved nearer to Goat, who had stopped cutting the grass. Goat had made up his mind that the work was too hard. He stood there resting, his eyes half closed. Suddenly Anansi swept Goat into his bag. Woodpecker, flying overhead a few moments later, saw Anansi's bag and broadcast, "Anansi's bag is nearly full. He is ahead of Monkey now." It was difficult to believe that Anansi had cut more grass than Monkey. Everyone could see that he was slower, yet his bag was almost full.

Tiger Cat looked at Monkey's bag, then at Anansi's. There was no doubt about it, Anansi was ahead. Then his eyes almost fell out of his head. The grass in Anansi's bag was moving. It was jumping about inside the bag. It seemed to be alive. He called out, "Old Woman Crim! Old Woman Crim!

What magic is this? What have you done to the
grass in your field? Look, it's moving, it's alive!"

Dry Bones hurried across the field, his long dry
joints creaking and groaning as he moved. Old
Woman Crim ran toward Anansi and Tiger Cat,
her long bent nose gleaming in the sunshine. Dog
and Monkey raced to the spot. Tiger Cat was scared.
He kept pointing and shouting, "The grass is bewitched! It's bewitched! It's alive!"

Dry Bones caught up the bag. The grass inside heaved and tossed in this direction and that.
Dry Bones threw the bag into the air and let it fall

to the ground. Goat jumped out, shouting, "You nearly broke my neck, you clumsy good-for-nothing! You nearly broke my neck. What do you mean by putting me in that bag?"

"Where's Anansi?" shouted Tiger Cat. "Where's Anansi?"

Goat shouted, "Find Anansi, find Anansi! I will deal with him." Goat looked around, Old Woman

Crim looked around, everyone hunted all around, chasing through the field, running this way and that. For twenty minutes, for half an hour they searched, but there was no Anansi. At the end of half an hour Old Woman Crim said, "It's no good! You have to watch Anansi all the time. If you don't, he takes the shape of a spider and escapes!" Overhead, in the branches of a tree that cast its shadow

across Old Woman Crim's house, a spider was busy
spinning its web.

"Yes," said Capuchin, "Anansi is a good watchman,
but we will have to watch our watchman closely."

And Brown Owl said, slowly and a little sadly,
"That is the end of the story, the end of the evening,
and the end of the party."

About the Authors

Philip Manderson Sherlock was born in Jamaica. At an early age he became a schoolteacher, and later secretary of the Institute of Jamaica, a cultural center with one of the finest collections of Caribbeana in the world. As a member of a United Kingdom Committee on Higher Education in the West Indies, he assisted with planning and starting the University of the West Indies. He was a member of the University Faculty for twenty-one years, and Vice Chancellor from 1963–1969. He was knighted by Queen Elizabeth II in 1967; was awarded the Gold Musgrave Medal of the Institute of Jamaica for his work in history and literature; and has received honorary degrees from several British and North American universities. He is now Secretary-General of the Association of Caribbean Universities.

Philip Sherlock's interest in Caribbean folklore began when he was a small boy living in a Methodist manse in a remote Jamaican village. The storytellers of the village were old Cookie Crawford, who was always quarrelsome by day but made up for it by telling stories at nightfall, and Tata John, the coachman. These wonderful storytellers led him as a child into the world of the animals, of Anansi the Spider Man, Iguana and little Firefly, and of *Ears and Tails and Common Sense,* and he has stayed there ever since.

Hilary Sherlock grew up in Jamaica and in Trinidad, where she heard the Anansi and Crick Crack stories for the first time. She surrounded herself with books and pet animals, among them a pig, a dog, and a cat named Moonshine. She has always been interested in teaching and in the first two R's, but she says, she had "neither liking nor aptitude for 'rithmetic."

She was graduated from Oberlin College and later studied at Bank Street College of Education. She currently teaches in London. She is especially interested in the adjustment of West Indian children to life in England.

About the Illustrator

Aliki Brandenberg grew up in Philadelphia and was graduated from the Philadelphia College of Art. Shortly after graduation she took her first trip, which was to Barbados. She spent an unforgettable summer there, and ever since, the West Indies have had a special meaning to her. Some of the research for the drawings for *Ears and Tails and Common Sense* came from her Barbadian sketchbook.

Aliki now fills other sketchbooks in Europe, where she spends summers traveling with her husband, Franz Brandenberg, and children, Jason and Alexa. The rest of the time the Brandenbergs live in New York City, where Aliki writes and illustrates books for children and bakes bread for her family.